YOU CAN FIND TEACHERS

Finding, Motivating, and Keeping Teachers – A Step-by-Step Guide for Church Leaders

Yvonne Stewart

Abingdon Press

YOU CAN FIND TEACHERS: A STEP-BY-STEP GUIDE

Copyright © 1988 by Abingdon Press

Third Printing 1991

All rights reserved.
The purchase of this book entitles the buyer to duplicate pages 24-30 and 37-47 as needed for use in the church. No other part of this work may be reproduced or transmitted in any form or by any means, electronic or mechanical, including photocopying and recording, or by any information storage or retrieval system, except as may be expressly permitted by the 1976 Copyright Act or in writing from the publisher. Requests for permission should be addressed in writing to Abingdon Press, 201 Eighth Avenue South, Nashville, TN 37203.

This book is printed on recycled, acid-free paper.

Library of Congress Cataloging-in-Publication Data

STEWART, YVONNE.
You Can find teachers.
(Called to serve series)
Bibliogrpahy: p.

ISBN 0-687-04605-X (pbk.: alk. paper)

1. Sunday-school teachers. I. Title, II. Series.
BV1534.S77   1988   268'.3   88-917

Scripture quotations in this publication, unless other noted, are from the *Good News Bible*, the Bible in Today's English Version. Copyright © American Bible Society, 1976. Used by permission.

Scripture quotations noted ILL are from *The Inclusive Language Lectionary*. Copyright © 1987 by the Division of Education and Ministry of the National Council of Churches Cooperative Publication Association.

Scripture quotations noted NIV are from the HOLY BIBLE; NEW INTERNATIONAL VERSION. Copyright © 1973, 1978, 1984 by the International Bible Society. Used by permission of Zondervan Bible Publishers.

MANUFACTURED IN THE UNITED STATES OF AMERICA

To Bunny Stewart and Marlene Wilson for their dedicated work on behalf of volunteers.

CONTENTS

INTRODUCTION 5

I. START WITH THE BASICS 6
    Know What You Are Asking People to Do 6
    Know Who You Need 8
    Establish a Recruiting System 9
    Obtain Official Support 12
    Set Up the Committee 12

II. HOW TO GET WHO YOU NEED 14
    Find Out Who You Have, Then Who You Need 14
    The Search 16
    Attracting More Volunteers 17
    If All This Doesn't Produce "Enough" Teachers 20
    When You Have "Enough" Teachers 22

III. RECOGNITION, DEVELOPMENT, AND SUPPORT 31
    Before Starting 32
    At the Beginning of the Work 33
    Throughout the Term 33
    At the End of the Term 35
    At the End of the Time of Service 35
    Can You Fire a Teacher? 36

FURTHER READING 36

INTRODUCTION

This booklet is written for people responsible for recruiting volunteer leaders for educational programs in the church—Christian education committees, order of ministry staff, Christian education directors, Sunday school superintendents, recruiting or nominating committees—to help you recruit, support, and train capable teachers in an effective and positive way. It starts from square one, assuming that you are organizing yourselves for the first time—or with a new resolve—to undertake an intentional recruiting campaign and process for teacher support and training.

The title indicates that this is a "step-by-step guide." This phrase may summon up images of easy-to-use instruction booklets for assembling backyard swings or repairing your own bicycle. You will find that this booklet is not quite like that. While I hope that the steps are laid out in a straightforward and logical way (unlike some assembly manuals), they cannot be applied to your congregation in the same way as one can apply directions to a brand-name, uniformly constructed swing set or bicycle. Congregations come in different sizes and exist in various settings—urban, rural, suburban, small town—and are affected by many factors—economic, social, and political. They are part of denominations that recommend particular governing structures—boards, sessions, committees, and so on. So an extra step is implicit in this guide, a step in which you, the reader, will assess the ideas in this booklet with your own common sense and apply them in ways that will work best in your situation.

Whatever their differences, congregations have a common call to educational ministry. Scripture contains many injunctions about telling the story: "In times to come your children will ask you. . . . Then tell them . . . " (Deut. 6:20-21); "Go quickly, now, and tell his disciples" (Matt. 28:7); "Take the teachings that you heard me proclaim . . . entrust them to reliable people, who will be able to teach others also" (II Tim. 2:2). We Christians need to hear and to pass on the Judeo-Christian story so we know who we are and how we are to live in God's world doing God's will—just as we need to know all about our families and about how to act as a member of those families in the community. It will not be easy for the Church to survive as an identifiable community of faith or to continue to do God's work unless the story is passed on through education.

Since education is so vital to congregational life, it seems appropriate that it be undertaken by the most capable and the most gifted people possible. We don't usually ask a poor singer (even though he or she may be a terrific person) to be a soloist in the choir. Neither should we ask anyone to teach who does not have the talent and the willingness to develop and use it. This is where you come in. Your job is to recruit those gifted people on whom much of the future of the Church depends.

I often hear recruiting committee members worrying about whether they will get enough teachers. Do you share this concern? I believe you can do so, but you might need to think differently about the word *enough*. As long as you find the best possible teachers in your congregation, you have "enough." You may not have enough names to write beside each position—"There's no one to teach the Grade Ones or the Youth Group"—but if the gifted people have been recruited, they, because of their skills, will find a way to organize so that there are learning opportunities for all (combining grades, setting up interest centers, and so on).

If you concentrate on "enough" instead of "best," your thinking might naturally tend this way: "We need to find fifteen people to lead fifteen classes from nursery age to adult every Sunday morning at 10:00 A.M. for ten months a year." And you might look primarily for people to fit into this arrangement. When you've finished recruiting, you may be fortunate to have gifted teachers, but you may also get people whose chief qualification is that they are available at that particular time. If you don't have the most suitable teachers, your organization won't accomplish what it is set up for—education, telling God's story.

Ideally, I am providing guidelines in this booklet to help you recruit the "best" teachers and "enough" of them to suit your present system, but my priority is always to help you find the people in your congregation and community with the God-given talents to undertake the essential task of telling the story of God and God's people. I also offer ideas of what to do with these gifted people once you have found them. You won't keep them if you don't provide training, support, and recognition of those front-line workers—an essential part of your congregation's educational ministry.

CHAPTER ONE
START WITH THE BASICS

- **Know What You Are Asking People to Do**
- **Know Who You Need**
- **Establish a Recruiting System**
- **Obtain Official Support**
- **Set Up the Committee**

The one who proclaims God's message speaks to people and gives them help, encouragement, and comfort. The one who speaks in strange tongues helps only himself, but the one who proclaims God's message helps the whole church.
. . . You must try above everything else to make greater use of those which help to build up the church (I Cor. 14:3-4, 12)

KNOW WHAT YOU ARE ASKING PEOPLE TO DO

To get started in organizing to recruit volunteer teachers effectively, you need to bring together some people to think and to talk about what needs to be done. If you are concerned about the way teachers are recruited in your congregation, approach the Christian education committee or go to the Sunday school superintendent or some teachers or the minister—whoever is suitable in your situation—and ask to discuss the issues.

When you meet, after getting to know one another, your interests, and concerns and agree that you want to improve your system of recruiting and supporting teachers, you need to develop a clear *statement* of what you are asking volunteer teachers to do, a *description* of what kind of teachers you want, and a *proposal* for a system to recruit teachers. Then you need official approval of the system before you begin recruiting. This may sound like a general and theoretical task that may be frustrating to do when you are faced with a dire need for teachers. Taking time to think about these basics will provide a focus to your work and to your congregation's educational ministry, and it will save time in the long run.

First, let's look at what you are asking leaders to do. That sounds straightforward enough, doesn't it? Teach, of course. But teach to what end? People want to feel that they are contributing to an exciting and important enterprise. They don't want to teach because, "There won't be a Sunday school if people like you don't volunteer." They don't want to volunteer just to keep something going for its own sake. They want to use their talents in a satisfying way that meets their needs and accomplishes something for others.

The most common complaint among unsatisfied volunteers working in the church or elsewhere is that they aren't given a clear purpose or goals for their work. The implication of this for you is that in order to recruit committed and capable teachers you have to be able to tell potential leaders what the overall purpose for education in your church is in a way that captures their imagination. As well, a recruiting committee needs to provide candidates for teaching with specific goals regarding the particular classes you're asking them to lead and the subject matter they will be dealing with. Since we are not at the recruiting stage yet, we will start with the overall purposes for teaching.

So what is it that you are asking educational leaders to do? First, what are you not asking them to do? You are not asking them to do their duty because they "should." You are not asking them to do an easy job—"Just follow the curriculum. It's all there. You just have to glance at it before you go to class."

You are asking people to be part of an essential task in the community of faith: education. Through teaching, people are introduced to the story and life and actions of the community of faith. Through education, people can deepen their commitments to God, to God's people, and to God's world.

You are asking teachers to:

● **pass on the heritage of our community of faith as it is set forth in scripture, worship practices, doctrine, and the Church's history of action in the world;**

- **present this story of faith in such a way that it can be understood by people according to their abilities and life experiences;**
- **invite people to "know" God through Jesus, to commit themselves more deeply to the community of faith, to live "as if" the commonwealth or kingdom of God were here now, where all people are equal recipients of God's love, mercy, and justice.**

In other words, you are asking teachers to be disciples, to do as Jesus the rabbi did. Jesus not only told the Hebrew story, but he also brought new insights and experiences to it. He told the story in ways that were relevant to the people, be they farmers or fishing folk, talking about God's nature and work in terms of sowing seeds or catching fish. Jesus taught so that people could decide to repent—to change their ways—to loving God, self, and neighbor and showing that love in all they do as part of the Christian community and in all of God's creation

In a phrase, you are asking teachers to be part of an exciting task—telling people that God through Jesus has changed the world and inviting them to continue to change the world as part of the community that walks with Jesus. (See below for an example of a congregation's purpose statement.)

Christian Education: A Life-time Curriculum*

The purpose of Christian education in the Church is to help persons of all ages come to know, to love, and to serve God as revealed in Jesus Christ. Motivated and strengthened through the community of the Church, each is enabled to develop Christian values for living.

The aim of our program is to help persons grow in Christian faith so that they may live joyously from birth through death. We foster a Christian identity that gives perspective and unity to the many activities in which each engages. Christian education continues from the cradle to the grave; the nurturing and growing never cease; the generations have much to share with one another.

The love of God is experienced through warm and caring relationships in home, church, and community. Knowledge about God, Jesus, and our biblical heritage is presented at appropriate stages in each person's development. Thus through a developing process of relationships, instruction, and involvement, Christian faith is nurtured.

---
*Reprinted by permission of Deer Park United Church, Toronto, Canada.

Jesus summarized the "greatest commandment," saying: " 'Love the Lord your God with all your heart, with all your soul, and with all your mind'; and 'Love your neighbor as you love yourself' " (Luke 10:27). On the surface this sounds so simple—but it has within it the essence of a life-time curriculum!

This task is not only exciting and creative, but also vital and challenging. It is vital because in these times God's world and God's people are in danger from so many unjust and unloving forces—militarism, pollution, greed, oppression—you name it. It is challenging because thre are so many other stories for people to listen to as well as the Judeo-Christian one, some leading to God and others not. Christianity is not picked up by osmosis in Western culture anymore. We Christians are part of a multi-cultural and secular society and must take full responsibility for doing a thorough job of teaching the Christian story to our community of faith and seeking commitment to the community and its work for the sake of our own and the world's God-given abundant life.

These general statements are presented here because you need to ask people not only to offer their particular gifts for a specific task, such as teaching music with the primary children, but also to commit themselves to a vision of the ultimate purpose of their efforts. The foregoing was intended to give you an expression of that vision. What is your vision? What would you say about the purpose of education in your church that would inspire the gifted people in your congregation to teach? Write your ideas here:

_____
_____
_____
_____
_____
_____
_____
_____
_____
_____
_____
_____
_____

KNOW WHO YOU NEED

When a recruiting committee is finally established, it will be important for them to identify specific requirements for teachers, such as being skilled in drama and able to work with youth. But your preliminary discussion group needs to establish the basics. First you need to know what kind of people you need to fulfill the purposes of teaching. Your group might brainstorm many ideas and then develop an outline that contains some of the following elements.

You need people who are:

- **Gifted as teachers**—or at least willing to discover whether they are.

    Usually you need people who have a flexible teaching style. A good teacher helps all members of a group learn by offering a variety of learning opportunities, since people learn in many different ways. These learning opportunities may include sitting and listening, doing things, solving problems, or researching and thinking. You may have groups who are together because they have a similar learning style; for example, they all like lectures. In this case, you probably need someone who predominantly teaches in this way.

    This may lead you to think that you need people who are professional teachers and that your recruiting committee will need to be scientific in its methods. You don't necessarily need professionals as teachers in the church. Unfortunately, they don't always have the gift for teaching, and, if they do, they often want a break on Sunday. Or they teach subject matter, such as accounting, that is so different that their skills may not apply to the education task of the Church. (This is not meant as a put-down of accounting teachers. They may also have the gift to tell God's story.)

    You also don't necessarily need personnel experts on your recruiting committee, but you do need people who are sensitive and observant and can match people's gifts with jobs.

    So how does one know if people have this gift of teaching? There is an art to this, but most of us do have intuitive ways of recognizing gifts in others. How many times do we hear people say that a young person will make a good artist or teacher or mechanic? How do people come to these conclusions?—by thinking about what they observe the young people saying, doing, and producing.

    So to identify gifted teachers, you need to observe people carefully to see if they demonstrate the qualities of good teachers in their everyday lives. Do they explain things clearly in ordinary conversation? Do they make sure their listeners understand them? Do they listen well? Do they speak so that everyone in a group can hear them? Do they like to learn new things, and can they interest others in them? Do they like to relate faith to life, and can they get others involved in doing so? Do they communicate in creative ways—through stories, skits, poems, and so on? Are they interested in people, in children, in youth?

- **Trying in what they say and do to live as a companion of Jesus**—loving and serving others, seeking to live in the world according to God's will.

- **Enthusiastic about studying scripture, church tradition, and history**—like to share learnings with others and relate them to today's world.

- **Open to God and others**—through prayer and community worship.

- **Sensitive to the needs of others**—they can live and share God's story in ways that are meaningful for the members of the group.

    Sometimes it may be more important for the class to attend to a pastoral concern in the group than to a discussion of a biblical theme.

For instance, when members learn that one of them is terminally ill, the teacher must be able to realize that it is more important to discuss this news in the light of their faith than the material he or she had prepared.

- **Creative**—teachers help people explore the faith in many different ways (through story, drama, art, film, research, music, meditation, humor, outreach) and relate it meaningfully to their lives. For instance, a class could learn a great deal by acting out a contemporary version of the parable of the good Samaritan and identifying the modern-day outcasts (Samaritans) who are ministering to the wounded "in group" of society today.

- **Courageous**—the gospel is meant to make the comfortable uncomfortable and the uncomfortable comfortable.

It is usually easier to comfort the uncomfortable parts of ourselves. The comfortable parts don't like to be disturbed and may react angrily if they are. And so it may be difficult for teachers to tell people that Jesus calls us to change our comfortable ways for the sake of others (as well as ourselves), especially when our culture reinforces our life-style. For example, some class members may not like to hear a leader say that even though society encourages accumulation of material wealth, especially if we worked hard to earn it, scripture tells us that we are blessed by God's action (rather than deserving), and God requires us to share our blessings (see Deut. 14:22-29, 15:4-18). It takes courage to present the disturbing gospel. Jesus knew all about that.

Some of these qualities apply to all Christians, some more specifically to teachers in the church. Are there other characteristics that you would seek in teachers? Write them here:

_____
_____
_____
_____
_____

_____
_____
_____
_____
_____
_____
_____
_____
_____
_____
_____
_____
_____
_____

You might worry whether people would be willing to volunteer when they see such a list of qualities. I believe there are people who have these characteristics in every congregation. They are not threatened by such standards, but are rather challenged by them. These are the people you want. Setting standards indicates that the job is an important one and one that needs to be done by the people with the gifts to do it.

ESTABLISH A RECRUITING SYSTEM

Once you've clarified the purpose of education in the church and identified the caliber of people required, you need to develop the best possible system to find such people to do the specific tasks in your education program. This is as far as you should go in your work as a discussion group before you seek official support for your ideas from appropriate church bodies.

There is not one single system that will work for every congregation, but there are basic tasks to be accomplished by any recruiting body. These are as follows:

- **Maintain a record of the gifts and interests of the congregation that relate to educational programs.**

Whether one person does this in a small congregation or a committee in a larger one, there needs to be a new consciousness of the interests and gifts members of the congregation have for educational ministry. This record can be kept in ways that are appropriate to your situation—in someone's notebook, which is made available to people seeking teachers, or in a sophisticated card or computer file that is kept in the church office.

- **Keep track of the needs for leadership in educational programs.**

  The person or committee responsible for recruiting should not wait passively for requests for leaders but rather take initiative, noting in board or committee minutes or conversations after church whether new groups needing leadership are being formed and whether present leaders are ill or overworked and need help or are moving and will need replacements.

- **Use the records to discover potential leaders.**

  In a large congregation, a recruiting committee member may need to do careful research through time and talent records to identify suitable candidates for particular educational tasks.

- **Prepare job descriptions of all education positions.**

  Even if your congregation has only one or two teachers for the entire Sunday school, it is still appropriate and considerate to outline their responsibilities. Giving them a job description lets them know that you value their work.

- **Promote the need for teachers in the congregation.**

  This will usually be a seasonal task, but there may be times throughout the year when new positions or vacancies may need to be filled.

- **Interview candidates and make recommendations regarding their suitability.**

  This could be a complex task in a large congregation, since there may be more than one candidate for many of the positions available. A recruiting committee will need to have members who are skilled in interviewing or to call on appropriate members of the congregation to help with this particular task for a specified period of time. In a small congregation, the process will involve a more informal conversation with people who may be neighbors or relatives, nevertheless it is one that is clearly focused on each person's ability and interest to serve as a teacher.

- **Prepare contracts or covenant forms.**

  No matter how many or few educational leaders are recruited, they and the congregation need to make a concrete expression of their commitments to educational ministry. Written contracts or covenants are one way of doing this.

  When you design a recruiting system for your particular situation, it is helpful to consider a time line within which the tasks need to be done. Having such a time line as the one outlined below helps both the recruiting committee (or person) and the people involved in Christian education to think, ahead, to plan, and to fulfill their responsibilities on time. Not all the items listed on this time line are the responsibility of the recruiting committee, but the performance of them all will affect the recruitment process, as further discussions will indicate.

TIME LINE FOR TEACHER RECRUITMENT AND SUPPORT

Two weeks before Palm Sunday	• Teacher evaluations and decisions whether to teach next year
Palm Sunday	• Recommitment breakfast for teachers and students
After Easter	• Meeting to identify teachers you have and how many you will need • Interviews of potential education leaders

Mid-May	• Finish recruitment or begin promotional recruitment campaign to fill remaining vacancies
End of June	• Finish promotion campaign • First meeting of new teachers • New teachers observe a class • Service of recognition for Sunday school leaders and students of the past year
Early September	• Dedication or covenant service for all teachers • Teachers' meeting for lesson planning • Weekly conversations with teachers as they begin their work
Ongoing	• Monthly teachers' meeting • One or two retreats or training sessions for leaders • Reports to committees, board, and congregation on the ongoing educational ministry

Following are stories from a variety of congregations. These congregations perform the tasks outlined above, using methods and time lines that work in their situations. Read these with an eye to the ideas that can work for you and that inspire your imagination to develop your own unique approach.

One small congregation had a special person who helped with all recruiting in the church. Her name was Olive. She made a point of talking with every visitor who attended Sunday worship. If they expressed any desire to continue to attend or any need for pastoral care, she visited them that week. Many, of course, continued to attend, and she continued to get to know them. Olive was a walking encyclopedia of the talents, needs, and interests of the congregation. So when the superintendent of the Sunday school needed teachers, she identified the tasks that needed to be done and then met with Olive to find out whom she knew who could do them. She and the superintendent shared the work of phoning and visiting potential candidates. The superintendent developed job descriptions to use during the visits and contracts for the people to sign when they decided to serve.

If you are part of a small church, you may already know of an Olive among you. All you might need to do is ask him or her to think more intentionally about potential teachers (or even make notes) and meet with them formally when appropriate.

An inner city church somewhat larger than Olive's has a recruiting committee that finds candidates for all positions in the church. It is made up of people who have a keen interest and expertise in recruiting procedures. To find leaders for educational programs, they work with the chairperson of the Christian education committee and the superintendent of the Sunday school. Committee members help them develop a system and a time line for identifying needs and help them write the job descriptions. Together, they identify potential candidates for the jobs.

The recruiting committee keep a card index of the talents and interests of as many congregational members as possible. These records are updated every year during the church's stewardship campaign, which emphasizes the giving of time and talent as well as money. One member keeps the file up-to-date and does the research when requests for volunteers are received.

Committee members write promotional material to go in the worship bulletin and newsletter when they need more people than they can find through the card index. The members team up with the Christian education chairperson and Sunday school superintendent to phone, visit, and interview potential teachers. Once people agree to serve as teachers, the committee members help them and the chairperson and superintendent to develop a contract that clearly states the expectations of all parties.

If your congregation is of an appropriate size, and if you have people in the congregation with talents in recruiting, perhaps this might be a system for you to consider. If your congregation is larger, here is another kind of organization to consider. The church in this story has many departments in its educational program and has a recruiting committee just for finding volunteer teachers. The committee is made up of the coordinators of all departments. Every spring, usually before Easter when people are often thinking about the renewal of faith commitments, the coordinators meet with all teachers to help them evaluate their educational ministry with their classes and to find out whether they are willing to teach next year. The coordinators meet right after Easter and share their lists of whom they will have again the next year and of whom they will need.

They keep a card index of all people in the congregation who've been asked to teach and the comments made, such as, "Ask me again when I've finished my thesis." First they select from the card file names of people whose talents match the jobs. They phone to set up an appointment and then make a personal visit. After a conversation to discover further the person's interests, they leave a statement of the purpose of education and of the qualities they seek in teachers and a specific job description for the person to reflect on. When individuals decide to serve, they are asked to sign a contract. If the committee still needs to find teachers after this process, they advertise in the worship bulletin and newsletter, clearly outlining the job and the specific requirements.

OBTAIN OFFICIAL SUPPORT

Your next step is to prepare a brief, clearly written report to present first to the Christian education committee, if you have one, and then to the session, or board or similar governing body. The report should indicate that you are seeking support in recruiting teachers because the work of capable teachers affects the ministry of the whole congregation, and this responsibility needs the support of its official bodies. Then give a statement of the purpose of education in the church and its importance today, a list of the qualities you seek in teachers, and an outline of the kind of committee or system you want for recruiting people who will fulfill these purposes.

The Christian education committee should see that you have time on the agenda to get the decision of the governing body on this matter. If possible, mail your report to board members in advance for reading and reflection. At the meeting itself, after introducing the report and its purpose, invite board members to talk in small groups of three or four for five or ten minutes and to note in writing where they agree and disagree with your ideas and what other ideas they have. Have a general discussion in the whole group, answering questions and responding to comments and concerns. Be sure to collect the written notes and promise to pass them on to the new recruiting committee for consideration. This process gives board or session members an opportunity to have some involvement in and ownership of the church's educational program.

The last and most important item of business is to ask for a decision to support your proposal to set up a recruiting system or committee. If the response is favorable, you can proceed with setting up a committee.

SET UP THE COMMITTEE

First you need to recruit the recruiters. Your system may automatically designate who the members will be (such as the Sunday school department coordinators). But no matter whether your committee membership is given or whether you need to seek it out, you need a job description, such as the one on page 13, so that people will be clear about their work on this particular committee. If your committee is made up of a designated group, you will need to discover whether you have within the group all the qualities necessary for the work of this committee. If not, recruit some additional people who have such qualities.

When the committee first meets, the members will need to take time to get to know one another and what talents each person has to help with the work. They may want to refine the job description to suit their particular talents and agreed upon style of working. For example, they may decide not to meet face to face weekly in the spring but rather communicate by computer bulletin board daily.

Whatever their talents and working styles, their main task will be to find appropriate leaders. The next chapter will provide some ideas to help with this important work.

Job Description for Recruiting Committee Member

Job Title: Recruiting Committee for Educational Leaders

Responsible to: the Session through the Christian Education Committee

Job Description: to set up and maintain a process for recruiting capable leaders for education programs.

Main Responsibilities:

- set up and maintain a record of the talents of congregational members related to educational ministry
- receive and seek out requests for leadership in educational programs
- find leaders using the records and appropriate promotion
- prepare job description
- interview candidates
- develop contracts or covenants

Time Required:

- weekly meetings in April, May, and June (meeting time would include time for interviews and phone calls)
- bi-monthly for the rest of the year
- some extra time for maintaining records, and so on

In-Service Training Provided:

- a day-long session with an expert in recruiting educational leaders
- opportunities and funds to attend workshops related to volunteerism

Qualifications and Special Skills:

- an interest and ability in matching people and jobs
- commitment to developing the best means of finding the best people for the jobs
- some understanding of our church's educational ministry
- experience or interest in keeping "Time and Talent" records
- ability to interview people and assess their skills
- good at developing promotional recruitment materials

Comments:

CHAPTER TWO
HOW TO GET WHO YOU NEED

- **Find Out Who You Have, Then Who You Need**
- **The Search**
- **Attracting More Volunteers**
- **If All This Doesn't Produce "Enough" Teachers**
- **When You Have "Enough" Teachers**

And passing along by the Sea of Galilee, Jesus saw Simon and Andrew the brother of Simon casting a net in the sea; for they were fishers. And Jesus said to them, "Follow me and I will make you become fishers of people." And immediately they left their nets and followed him. (Mark 1:16-18 ILL)

FIND OUT WHO YOU HAVE, THEN WHO YOU NEED

If you were recruiting players for a football team, you would first want to know what good players were being carried over from last year so that you would know which positions you would need to concentrate on filling and what kind of teammates you would need to complement present players.

A volunteer recruiting committee can do a much more effective job of finding appropriate teachers if they first find out who is serving already. Then they can look for people whose gifts balance with the talents of present teachers. Therefore, you need to establish a system and a time line for doing this. Perhaps you could adapt one of the systems outlined in the last chapter. The Sunday school superintendent or department coordinators could ask all teachers to indicate by Palm Sunday whether they wish to teach during the following year. (You also need to project how many students and classes there may be.) There could even be a special Palm Sunday recommitment breakfast for all those wishing to continue. (Their recommitment is a way of joyfully following Jesus on this particular Sunday.) At that time, they could fill out a recommitment form, something like the one on page 25. Students could fill one out, too.

When you know who you have, the superintendent and the coordinators could meet right after Easter to draw up a detailed list of people required, in the light of the talents and needs of the teachers already serving. For example, your first list might start like this:

Pat Jones needs a new teammate for her primary class. She's really good on background material and preparation of content. She is task oriented and works well with a relaxed, creative person, someone who can help the children deal with the subject matter through art, drama, and so on.

We need a music leader for Junior Assembly. The last one wasn't the best match—would teach hymns only and resisted any contemporary music. We need someone who is comfortable with both types of music and junior children. Maybe someone who could help put on a biblical musical.

We need someone to lead the fifties adult group. They've been together for twenty years. We need someone who appreciates the importance of the emotional aspects of the group life. They like experiential-type Bible study that relates to life today.

Job Descriptions

This list will help you to know exactly what gifts you need in people and will help you prepare specific job descriptions. There may be one person in the group who likes to do this, or each coordinator could write the job descriptions related to his or her department. It is probably best for you to have a common general outline of job descriptions for the writers to fill in the requirements specific to each position. In the sample on page 15, the elements in bold type form a core outline; the other elements provide specifics.

Job Description for Sunday School Teacher

Job Title: Sunday School Teacher
Primary Class

Responsible to: the Church Board through the Christian Education Committee

Main Responsibilities: teaching the Christian story in thoughtful and creative ways that people can understand and that invite them to live out God's will in the Christian community and in God's world.

Particular Responsibilities:
- teach a primary class
- organize creative activities, particularly drama and crafts, that involve the children and illustrate lessons
- prepare each session in collaboration with a teammate
- content of lesson
- gathering supplies
- room set up
- lead the class with a teammate
- clean up after sessions
- evaluate the sessions with the children, teammate, and department coordinator

Time Required:
- two hours per Sunday for ten months, September to June (one hour lesson, one half hour setup, one half hour cleanup and evaluation)
- two hours per week preparation
- three hours per month teachers' meetings and training sessions
- two full days per year, one in October and one in May, for planning or training

Qualifications or Special Skills
- ability to work with boys and girls in Grades 1, 2, and 3
- talent in crafts and drama
- student of scripture and the Christian faith
- able to relate the faith to the children's lives through the arts
- able to work with a teammate, whose talent is for thorough preparation and enabling the children to research facts and information

In-Service Training Provided:
- monthly teachers' meeting and training sessions
- two full days per year of training and planning regarding topics of the teachers' choice
- funds available to attend training events at church training centers
- extensive library of resource books to help in lesson preparation as well as extensive supplies for creative and audio-visual equipment

In my opinion, job descriptions are as important for volunteers as they are for those who get paid to work. Volunteer tasks fulfill important functions in the church and society and need to be treated as if they do. Providing job descriptions is one way of indicating to the volunteers that their work is valuable.

With a job description before them, potential volunteers know what the job entails, what is expected of them, and what support they will receive. They will know that they have standards to live up to and that the institution they serve (in this case the church) is obliged to help them do the best job possible.

Some people may back off from volunteering when they see formal job descriptions, but capable people are usually *more* willing to volunteer if they know what is expected of them. Therefore, job descriptions can help you screen recruits. Later on these job descriptions are a valuable reference when you help teachers evaluate their work.

Job descriptions also provide volunteers with something concrete to consider. Volunteers are not just being asked to do a vague task called teaching but to use their particular talent to do a specific teaching job. People like to know how much time is required for volunteer teaching. If the job description mentions only one hour every Sunday, they may not be pleased to learn later that they are also expected to spend time in lesson preparation and to attend monthly teachers' meetings and at least one weekend training event. Although you may not foresee all the time expectations, it's best to outline them as fully as possible.

Also, potential teachers like to know the length of time they are expected to teach. In some congregations, it is almost implicit that once you have volunteered to teach, you're in it until you're worn out. People are more likely to respond when there is a stated term of teaching on the job description, be it a semester of six weeks or a full year. Some congregations suggest three-year terms—one to learn, one to act on the learnings, and one to train another teacher.

Recruiting committees need to know what benefits come with the job and to list them on the job description. People who want to do the job well will be reassured and attracted when they know that there are helps such as funds for training events at lay training centers, workshops in the congregation, a resource library, and audio-visual equipment and materials.

THE SEARCH
Preparation
Make a succinct list of teacher requirements, such as

- **primary teacher, creative arts**
- **easy-going junior music leader, knowledge in contemporary and traditional music**
- **adult leader, good at community building and experiential Bible study.**

Then brainstorm a list of names of people who are suitable for each job. Recruiting Committee members could also contact other members of the congregation to add to the list by asking them pertinent questions, such as: Who is good in drama with children? Who works well with questioning young people? Who likes to lead in-depth adult study and interpretation of scripture?

Implicit in these questions is a concern about the appropriateness of people to work with different age groups or with different ways of learning and believing. For example, people who talk about abstract concepts, such as love and justice, without illustrating them in concrete terms would not be appropriate teachers for primary children, who think concretely. (They might not be suitable to work with some adult groups either, who may have just as much trouble with abstract thinking.) People who have never questioned their faith and are upset by people who do would probably be unsuitable as leaders of deeply questioning youth or adults, but may work well with young children or others who enjoy learning the stories of our faith for their own sake. Be sure to keep this kind of matching in mind as you list requirements and interview candidates.

Go over the list and decide who on the committee will contact people for which positions and agree on the order in which potential candidates for each position will be approached. Before making contacts, if you have never kept records before, prepare forms or cards that can be filled in after interviews and put into a time and talent index. See page 26 for card format sample.

If a congregation really wants to make it clear that they value people before jobs, the recruiting or stewardship or pastoral care committee could interview all church members first to find out what they consider their talents to be and where they want to use them in the church. Then match the people to the necessary jobs, or even adapt the jobs to suit the people.

If you are starting with jobs first, as we are here,

the best way is to identify the talents needed for specific tasks and then seek out the suitable people. This approach helps people feel that their gifts are appreciated. A person is more likely to respond positively if asked to lead an adult group when he or she is recognized for having the considerable knowledge and leadership ability required for experiential Bible study, rather than if asked to volunteer to teach simply because teachers are needed.

Interviews

If possible, even the first contact should be made in person. A coffee hour after Sunday worship is an opportunity to seek out potential candidates for a brief conversation. Tell them what gifts you think they have and for what job. Ask them if they would consider talking further about the prospect of volunteering to teach. If they say yes, make an appointment to see them in their homes or at church, whatever is suitable, during the next week. Give them a copy of the statement of the purpose of education, the qualities needed in Sunday school teachers and the job description for the specific job you are asking them to consider. If you can't see these people, phone them and either mail out the material or drop it off before you visit them with a note saying you are looking forward to your time together.

When you visit with the candidates, make it clear that you will take a specified period of time, for example, no longer than an hour. Emphasize again the gifts the person has and how you see that person contributing significantly to the church's educational ministry. Ask if he or she has any questions. If you use a curriculum, it is helpful to bring a sample, in case there are questions related to content. You may also bring a class list, if the person wants an idea of whom he or she may be working with. Listen attentively. Respond to questions and concerns as best you can. Treat these doubts seriously and be realistic. People know that teaching has its ups and downs, and they want to know what support they'll have.

You, on the other hand, will want to find out more about the person's interest and experience in working with the particular age group and about special talents, such as music or art, and how they may be used with this age group. Discuss the person's views on the purpose and content of the subject matter to be taught, be it a laid-out curriculum or teacher-developed material to suit the particular group.

Toward the end of your time together, you may have a sense of whether it is appropriate to ask for a decision then. If it is, and the person says yes, explain that all teachers are asked to sign a covenant form or contract (see the sample on pages 29-30). Give the person a copy and suggest that she or he take a day or so to fill it out. Set a definite time for the person to deliver it to the church or for you to pick it up. If this is not the appropriate time, suggest that the person take another forty-eight hours to think it over; explain and leave a covenant form and arrange a definite time and way to receive the reply and/or the covenant form.

This process may seem to take a long time, but it's well worth it. Taking time conveys to people the message that they are important, that the job they are being asked to do matters, and that care must be taken to find the right person for the job and the right job for the person. This applies whether you are in a tiny rural church, an inner city church, or a burgeoning suburban one.

Follow Up

The recruiting process described thus far is the best way to recruit the "best" teachers. Even if the people you approach don't all agree to serve, you've had an opportunity to get to know people in your congregation and to let them know that their gifts are appreciated and needed. Some people may want to teach, but can't manage it this year. Others may not want to teach, but do want to do something else. Be sure to make notes on the cards you've created and pass on information about willing volunteers to appropriate committees.

The recruiting committee should aim to complete this interview process by mid-May, if possible.

ATTRACTING MORE VOLUNTEERS

Besides approaching individuals, as described so far, you probably will want to launch a congregation-wide campaign to attract volunteer teachers. You will still be seeking people to fill *specific* jobs, not simply asking for teachers "in general." A recruiting campaign over the next four to six weeks (mid-May to the end of June) should help you fill in the remaining open teaching positions. This kind of promotional effort will encourage people whose gifts are not known to the recruiting committee to come forward. You may also find a number of people who will not fill existing openings, but will be good resources in the future.

Effective Promotion

Your campaign message will be better communicated to potential teachers if you have a focus that is presented effectively in visual, written, and oral ways.

The statement "Your Gift Can Co a Long Way," paired with a picture of the loaves and fishes, carries a strong biblical message and conveys the conviction that the reader's talent or gift is special. Each person's unique gift *does* make a difference. In using our gifts, we are following Jesus' example and serving God's people.

On pages 43-47, you will find the Loaves and Fishes design in several sizes. The design may be reproduced to make posters, flyers, newsletter and bulletin announcements, or a special letterhead. Use this logo along with the statement "Your Gift Can Go a Long Way" or alternative statements (also provided in reproducible form on pages 43-47) to develop your own church-wide campaign for teachers.

This statement and logo can be used in many ways to communicate the need for teachers and the opportunity for people to make a difference in the life of the church. Here are some examples of ways to develop your promotional campaign around this theme.

Stories in Church

During announcement time in church, have satisfied teachers tell their stories. Ask them to refer to the logo or slogan and talk about how they felt that their gifts counted. They could explain why they chose to teach, how they used their talents with their classes, or what they learned and experienced. Most important, they will invite members of the congregation who think they have the gift for teaching and are committed to the purposes of education in your church to join in the challenging task of education. Each speaker can outline the details of one or more of the available teaching positions.

After the service, the teachers and members of the recruiting committee could be available at the back of the church to answer questions and to arrange interviews with interested people.

A different teacher could tell his or her story on each of the four to six Sundays, and each could describe one or two of the specific teaching positions that are available. Doing this lets the congregation know not only that gifted people are needed to teach, but also that education is an important and satisfying ministry.

Notices in the Worship Bulletin or Newsletter

Make sure a request for volunteer teachers stands out visibly in the worship bulletin or newsletter. Use the logo to illustrate the written material each week so that people will recognize what the item will be about. If you repeat the visual, you may want to use different slogans or biblical references each week. Here are some possibilities:

- **Tomorrow Depends on You Today**
- **You Can Make a Difference**
- **Take Your Light out from Under a Bushel**
- **You Could Be the Spark**
- **Come and Build the Body of Christ**
- **Teach: Prepare Today's Disciples.**

This notice should emphasize that you are seeking people with the gifts of teaching and outline the details of the specific jobs available. You could also include quotations from satisfied teachers or brief biblical references. Always give the name and phone number of a contact person from the recruiting committee for interested people to call. If the notice is in the worship bulletin, you could also name a person and place where people could talk after church.

Bulletin Boards

Consider putting the logo on all church bulletin boards, especially in places where people linger before and after church services and meetings. It might even be appropriate to post it on community bulletin boards. Put under the poster a list and brief description of the specific teaching jobs available and a tear-off of the name and phone number of a contact person.

Letters to Teachers, Students, and Parents

All of these people could be helpful adjunct recruiters. Students often know what kind of teacher they learn best from. Parents have ideas about who would work well with their children and young people. Teachers may be willing to seek out suitable teammates. You could write to these people, explaining that you are still trying to find capable teachers and need their help. Describe the specific positions available or include the job descriptions and ask them to submit names of people who could do these jobs and fulfill the purposes of education in your church. Be sure to give the name and phone number of a contact person on the recruiting committee. (See the sample letters on pages 27-28.)

Appeal to What Motivates People

Your interviews and promotions should not only help people to recognize whether they have gifts for teaching and to challenge them to use those gifts, but also to let people know they will be able to use their gifts in ways suitable to them.

David McClelland and John Atkinson* identify three main types of motivations that affect people's work related behavior. Some people do things in life because they like to be connected with people—to care for them and be cared for. Others like to have a sense of accomplishment, of doing something well, and still others like to be a part of bringing about change in people and situations.

Many of us may be able to think of Sunday school teachers who had these different motivations. The one who remembered everybody's birthday and brought special treats on the Sunday nearest the day; who sent "get-well" or "I missed you" cards; who wanted to know whether all was well at home and school and celebrated or grieved accordingly represents the first type. Do you recall a teacher who put a lot of effort into preparing interesting lessons and encouraged you as you built models of Palestinian villages to learn about the details of life in Jesus' time or congratulated you on memorizing scripture passages so well? That's the second type. Do you remember the one who urged us to live life differently because of God's love and involved us in projects of visiting senior citizens' homes, hospitals, jails, and so on? That approach indicates the third type of person.

In using stories of satisfied teachers in your recruitment campaign, you can appeal to more people by choosing people whose stories reveal these different motivational styles. If people hear only about wonderful lesson plans, they will think that all teachers need to be best at this, rather than at building a caring community or helping to change attitudes and behavior. Students need to experience all these types of teachers, and you need to recruit them.

Knowing about differing motivations can help you to put together teams of teachers—if you have team-teaching in your Sunday school. A teacher who takes time to make sure that the children are cared about as individuals and that they care for one another may balance well with a teacher who is keen to involve the class in social outreach

---

*George H. Litwin and Robert A. Stringer, Jr. *Motivation and Organizational Climate* (Boston: Harvard University Press, 1968).

projects. So when you make up the list of teachers you need and when you interview, try to be aware of the need to appeal to and recruit people with different motivations.

IF ALL THIS DOESN'T PRODUCE "ENOUGH" TEACHERS

If You Have a Few Vacancies

If you are missing an adult leader here and a fifth-grade teacher there and there seems to be no prospect of finding anyone, you may be able to make some adjustments to the system.

If you have a shortage of teachers for children, consider combining some grades and have interest centers each week. One or two teachers plan the lesson and decide on the interest centers—such as crafts that illustrate a point in the lesson; reading and research in which children tape record their thoughts; and drama. If you have a mix of ages, the centers need to suit their abilities. For example, if you combine children in grade 1 with children in higher grades, you need to have one or two centers that don't require reading or sophisticated manual skills.

The recruiting committee could then find people to work with these teachers. Someone may come for a few weeks to help the children bake bread or make parchment paper or shoot a video *or* may assist on a long-term basis. These assistants may not have teaching skills, but by working with those who do, they can contribute much toward the education of the children.

One church that uses learning centers all the time incorporates cooking into the program each year—usually preparing treats for shut-ins. For many years, an elderly lady in the congregation came to teach the children how to make terrific fudge or cookies. She could never have taught Sunday school, but she sure could cook! The teachers always put her special contribution into the context of telling and living God's story. The woman is now dead and the children grown, but they still remember the fudge. She would never have given this gift if she hadn't teamed with effective teachers in a learning center program.

If you don't have enough leaders for youth and adults, combine groups under the coordination of a leader with good group skills. This leader can help some members of the group learn to be small group discussion and activity leaders. Then the teacher can present the focus or subject matter for the day to the whole group and small groups can discuss it or do related drama, art, and so on.

This kind of group could also bring in a series of leaders who would work with the one ongoing teacher. The class could decide what subjects they want to discuss or what interests they want to pursue and then seek out appropriate resource people. For example, they may decide to take two or three months to learn and put on a biblical musical, six weeks in a study of Isaiah, or two months on a social issue facing the Church today. If they use a curriculum, they could go through the topics in it and decide who they could bring in to help with certain units of the material. These resource people could be members of the congregation or people with particular knowledge and skills in the community. Bringing in people from outside the church provides an opportunity for an exchange of talents and points of view. The ongoing teacher can help the class put the contributions of the community people into the context of education in the church.

You might also want to think again about whether you've considered everybody in the congregation. You may have been thinking only of people who could come to the church to teach. Maybe you have shut-ins or physically disabled people who might not be comfortable in the church building but who are excellent teachers. If such people are willing, consider setting up a class in the person's home or institution *or* making the church building more accessible.

If You Have a Lot of Vacancies

This state of affairs may require some deep thinking and major changes. The recruiting committee should review all notes from interviews with potential candidates and make a list of reasons why people did not want to volunteer. The list might be something like this:

- **don't want to miss worship**
- **don't want to leave adult class**
- **haven't time to teach every Sunday**
- **don't know enough about the Bible**
- **don't know what to do when people ask questions about their faith.**

A common pattern may quickly appear. If not, it might be worth sponsoring an open meeting of the congregation to inform them of the lack of teachers and to discuss the reasons. Try to ensure that members of the Christian Education Committee, the Church Board, all people approached to teach, parents, and students attend. Ask them to discuss in small groups honestly why they don't want to teach, or why they think people don't want to teach, and share their findings in the whole group. Ask also for suggestions about what could be done to convince them to teach (assuming they have the ability).

Here are some solutions that congregations have come up with:

- **Changing Sunday school for children from the same time as worship to an hour before;**
- **Setting up regular study, prayer, and social meetings for teachers so that they will have an alternative to an adult class;**
- **Offering teachers a leave of one or two months so that they may attend the worship service or their adult class;**
- **Setting up a semester system in the Sunday school. The teaching material is organized into time blocks of six weeks or two to three months so that people can volunteer to teach for one or two semesters;**
- **Offering training in Bible study to teachers *or* approaching the Bible study group in the congregation to see if they have the interest and gifts to teach.**

What ideas might apply in your situation?

Whatever the problems, there *can* be solutions. The key is to be open enough to explore new possibilities and to be willing to change things from the way they've always been done.

One small rural congregation would not change. The parents were disatisfied with the Sunday school program for their children, and they couldn't get any volunteers to teach. Their program consisted of one class of all the children—ages four to eleven—that met at the same time as worship under the leadership of two young, loving, and inexperienced women. They really were providing babysitting instead of instruction.

First, the congregation tried to call in some of the church's conference staff to provide training for the present leaders, but the leaders were resistant and did not want to learn how to do anything differently. So the congregation asked the staff to help find a solution.

The conference staff took time to get to know the members. They identified two people with obvious teaching skills and asked why they weren't teaching. They weren't teaching because Sunday school was held at the same time as the worship service, which they didn't want to miss. Also, they were heavily involved in community activities, such as leading a drama group, and didn't want to give up their activities to teach for ten months of the year. Then they were asked if there were any circumstances under which they *would* teach. They responded that they would teach all the children in the congregation in a learning center program for two hours on Sunday afternoons for six weeks in the fall and six weeks in the spring as well as for one week of half-days in the summer. They had creative ideas for adapting the church curriculum to suit their situation.

The conference staff approached the parents and the church board with this asked for "solution." The board chose not to accept the proposal because they didn't want to change, even though they could have kept the babysitting program during worship. The idea was too different. They weren't sure they wanted the noise of play-acting and music and mess from arts and crafts in the Sunday school. And even though the suggested times were not inconvenient, they just couldn't see Sunday school in these time periods and so spread out. Maybe the staff people and the two talented teachers could have tried to adapt their ideas somewhat to suit those of the parents and the board. But the parents and the board definitely needed to think about the purpose of education, rather than the form, and about using the "best" teachers in their midst rather than those who fit into the present pattern. As a result of the board's decision, the children in this congregation will have practically no exposure to the story of our faith and its application to their lives.

Another congregation decided that they would change. Since they couldn't get enough teachers for the children's program, they provided training and resources for parents. The parents met in a class with the minister, who was a good educator, and discussed the resource material in the light of their own faith and in terms of how to use this material in their families. Sometimes all the "families" and interested congregation members met in the church hall for special learning and social occasions, such as having a Passover Seder meal. Even though all parents may not be gifted teachers, the parents' religious education class and the resources they were given helped them involve their children in the faith journey.

Some congregations, for the same reasons as those above, have instituted family cluster programs in which groups of adults, youth, and children learn together for a block of time under a trained leader—either someone from the congregation or someone paid for leading the sessions and training future leaders at the same time.

In some cases, congregations hire staff on a short- or long-term basis to provide ongoing training of potential teachers and of parents so that in time there will be people to recruit for a Christian education program. The excuse for not doing this, although sometimes valid, is that there is no money to hire such a person. This is surprising, considering how much adults pay for the great variety of lessons, and organizations that they and/or their children are involved in. Is it not important to have quality religious education—as well as music, dancing lessons, and sports activities?

Jesus upset the people in authority in his time because he was always putting people before systems. Although it may be necessary in our times to have a system for education in the church and a system for recruiting and supporting teachers in it, we must also remember that it is the people and their education that come first, and we must adapt the system to suit their situation and needs.

WHEN YOU HAVE "ENOUGH" TEACHERS

Covenant or Contract Forms

Earlier it was suggested that committed teachers sign contracts or covenant forms. See pages 29-30 for examples. These forms are not intended to add to the bureaucracy of our lives. We have enough forms to fill out. They are intended to make clear that the teacher is making a serious commitment; to outline what the teacher is committing himself or herself to and what the congregation is agreeing to provide; and to recognize that God is intended to be a third party to these promises.

Some congregations design and use contract forms that outline the conditions of work for teachers in the church, similar to a formal contract one may sign at the beginning of a paid job. This is helpful because expectations are clear on both sides.

However, it is more appropriate for teachers to recognize that their gift of teaching is God-given and that with God's help they will be using it to serve God and God's people in the educational ministry of a congregation. At the same time, the congregation will use its God-given community life and resources to cherish and develop the gifts of teaching among themselves with God's help. A form that conveys this message is more appropriately called a *covenant* form because God's presence and gifts are always part of the relationship.

Covenant Service or Service of Dedication

Teaching is not just an individual commitment. It is a commitment by a part of the body of Christ that has the gift of teaching to use it to serve the whole body of Christ. The community of faith, in turn, makes promises to this particular part of the body.

The best way to enact these community commitments in the presence of God is through worship. If you have "enough" teachers by the end of your recruitment campaign at the end of June, it is appropriate to complete the process with a covenant, or dedication service. Early September (when classes begin a new season) would probably be the most suitable time. Even if you have a semester system in which people teach for only two months per year, it is still best to recruit *all* teachers at the same time and to involve all of them in this worship service. Such a service helps the whole congregation to acknowledge its responsibility before God for the educational ministry of the church.

The Litany of Dedication on page 24 may give

you some ideas to adapt to your situation. The litany has been used effectively in regular worship, usually before the reading of the Word. If you don't have the Eucharist, or Communion, every Sunday, try to arrange to have the dedication service on a Communion Sunday. Communion emphasizes that all members of the body need nurture and feeding and that they receive it by God's action—God's action through Jesus and all who are part of the body of Christ.

A LITANY OF DEDICATION

Minister: Each of us is called by God to fulfill a ministry in the world. We are also called to offer such gifts as we are able within the church so that it may more effectively fulfill its ministry of worship, witness, and work. You are now offering yourselves for service in this congregation through leadership in the Sunday school. In the exercise of your responsibilities, you will need to continue to study and to grow in faith. Be diligent in your work, confident that this faith community will support you in love.

In the presence of God and before these children, youth, and adults, I ask you: Do you believe in your Creator, in Jesus Christ your Savior, and in the Holy Spirit, your teacher and guide?

(Answer: 'I do.')

Minister: Do you promise to be diligent in your preparation and faithful in your witness, that students may be helped to grow in the Christian faith?

(Answer: 'I do.')

Minister: Will you accept the responsibilities of this task?

(Answer: 'I will, God being my helper.')

Christian Education Committee Representative: On behalf of these teachers, I light this candle as a symbol of the promises we have made.

The Response of the Students:

First Candlelighter: I light this candle to remind us that regular attendance in our Sunday school is important.

Second Candlelighter: I light this candle to remind us that we are a part of a community of faith.

Third Candlelighter: I light this candle to remind us that through Jesus' life we are better able to understand God's love.

All the students will say together: We promise that we will endeavor to be regular in our attendance and faithful in our study, that we may grow in our knowledge of Jesus and be helped to walk in his way.

The parents of children in Sunday school will stand and say together: We parents welcome the teachers of our children. We pledge to you our prayers and our support by encouraging our children, by talking with them about Christian faith, and by providing homes in which they may learn both by word and by example.

A parent will come forward, light a candle, and say: On behalf of these parents, I light this candle as a symbol of our pledge this day.

Parents, teachers, and students will now covenant together, saying: We, in the presence of God, covenant together to endeavor to make this Sunday school a place in which we share our knowledge of God's love and where God's love will be experienced.

Minister: (or chairperson of church board or Christian education committee): On behalf of this community of faith, I install you as teachers in this Sunday school. May you find joy in your service.

Recommitment Forms

For Teachers:

I hereby recommit myself to the educational ministry of _____ Church. With God's help, and with the help of this congregation, I offer my gifts of teaching to _____ class for the months of _____.

_____
year

In Christian Service

_____
(signature)

Name: _____

Address: _____

Phone: _____

Date: _____

For Students:

I hereby recommit myself as a participant in the educational ministry of _____ Church. I expect to be a part of _____ class. With God's help and the companionship of the Holy Spirit, I seek to deepen my Christian faith.

Name: _____

Address: _____

Phone: _____

Date: _____

For Children:

I would like to come to Sunday school at _____ Church next year. I hope to be in _____ class to learn about God's love.

Name: _____

Address: _____

Phone: _____

Date: _____

Cards For Teacher Time and Talent File

Name: _____

Address: _____

Phone—Home: _____

    Business: _____

Occupation: _____

Why This Person Was Approached:

Talents That Could Be Used in Teaching:

Style of Teaching:

Age Group Preferences:

Subject or Curriculum Preferences:

Previous Experience in Sunday School Teaching:

Reasons for Volunteering:

Time Available for Teaching:

Reasons for Not Volunteering:

Other Volunteer Work in the Church That This Person Would Like to Do:

BULLETIN NOTICE

"Your Gift Can Go a Long Way"

If you have a gift for teaching, use it.

Jean Brown did. Here is her story.

"I knew I was good with children, and I loved telling stories. The recruitment committee convinced me I should use these abilities in Sunday school. I've been teaching a class of primary children for two years now and love it. The church has sponsored me to attend storytelling workshops. I've since been able to help other teachers improve their storytelling. The children love to hear Bible stories and are learning to tell and act them out themselves. We've learned a lot together about the Christian faith. I'm so glad I was asked to use my gifts. They've gone a long way."

What are your talents? Are you willing to use them in Sunday school? Do you want to make them "go a long way"? Here are some opportunities for teaching in our Sunday school. See where you might serve.

Kindergarten: a teacher for four- and five-year-olds, especially with music skills

Junior: two teachers—one interested in biblical research with this age; one with talent in arts and crafts

Youth: someone who relates well with youth, who accepts their questioning and rejecting of the faith and can challenge them to continue to struggle on the faith journey.

Adult: a teacher who is interested in social justice issues and can relate them to the Christian faith.

LETTER TO PARENTS

Dear _____,

This is the time of year when we recruit teachers for the _____ term. We have not been able to find
_(year)
teachers in the department(s) your child(ren) attend, and we need your help.

We are seeking primary teachers with gifts in:

- **lesson planning**
- **music**
- **storytelling**

If you know of anyone who has these talents for teaching, please call me with the name, address, and phone number of that person(s).

Thank you for helping us build a team of gifted teachers for your child(ren).

Name:
Address: _____
Phone: (Recruitment Committee Member)

LETTER TO TEACHERS

Dear _____,

This is the time of year for recruiting teachers for the _____ term. We need you to help us find
_(year)
your colleagues for you so that we can build a well-balanced, competent body of teachers for our Sunday school.

We are seeking teachers for:

Kindergarten: a teacher for four- and five-year-olds, especially with music skills

Junior: two teachers—one interested in biblical research with this age; one with talent in arts and crafts

Youth: someone who relates well with youth, who accepts their questioning and rejecting of the faith and can challenge them to continue to struggle on the faith journey.

Adult: a teacher who is interested in social justice issues and can relate them to the Christian faith.

If you know of anyone in the congregation with these gifts for teaching, please pass on the appropriate job description (enclosed) and then contact me so that I can meet with that person.

Thank you for your help.

Name:
Address: (Recruitment Committee Member)
Phone:

LETTER TO STUDENTS

Dear _____,

This is the time of year when we recruit teachers for the _____ term. We have not been able to find
_(year)
teachers for your class/department, and we need your help.

We are seeking teachers with these talents:

- **adult leader good at relating faith to life**
- **youth leader good at recreational programming**

If you know of anyone with these gifts of teaching and whom you would like as a teacher, please call me with the name, address, and phone number of that person.

Thank you for helping us find the best possible teachers for you.

Name:
Address: (Recruitment Committee Member)
Phone:

CONTRACT FORM

I _____ agree to teach _____ class from _____ to _____; to attend teachers' meetings as outlined in the job description; and to prepare lessons thoughtfully and prayerfully according to the purpose of education of _____ Church.

I understand that I will receive:

- **opportunities to develop my abilities for teaching in the church at regular teachers' meetings and other special events.**
- **curriculum, resource material, equipment and supplies, and assistance for lesson planning**
- **regular support and evaluation of my work**

_____ _____
              Signature   date

_____
      Christian Education Committee
              Chairperson

CONFIRMATION OF CONTRACT*

Dear _____,

Thank you for agreeing to teach in the _____ department from _____ to _____. It is good to know that you will be a member of the team. Your willingness to give of your time and talent to the Sunday school is greatly appreciated. Your department coordinator, _____, is looking forward to working with you. Do not hesitate to phone (tel. #   ) if you have any questions. The coordinators have scheduled dates to meet with each term's teachers. Please note the date for your meeting and write it in your appointment book now, to help avoid the problem of conflicting dates later on. Thank you for doing this.

      Dates: Term I   - Fall   - Thursday, September 10
               Term II - Winter - Thursday, December 10
               Term III - Spring - Monday, March 28

The dedication service for all church school teachers will take place during the morning service on Sunday, September 20. At this time, the congregation affirms our teaching ministry and acknowledges its support to us. We hope you will be able to be present for this important worship service.

Thank you for the commitment you have made to the Sunday school, and we assure you that the coordinators will do their best to support and to guide you in your work.

                                                  Sincerely,

_____ _____
                                      for the Coordinators.

*Reprinted by permission of Deer Park United Church, Toronto, Canada.

COVENANT FORM

A Letter of Call

[God] appointed some to be . . . teachers. He did this to prepare all God's people for the work of Christian service, in order to build up the body of Christ. And so we shall all come together to that oneness in our faith and in our knowledge of the Son of God. (Ephesians 4:11*b*-13)

We at _____ **Church,** as part of the body of Christ, covenant
- to teach the scriptures;
- to provide for instruction in the Christian tradition and faith;
- to nurture spiritual growth;
- to proclaim the good news;
- to support God's people as they serve the world.

We invite you, _____ , as a teacher
- to study scripture daily;
- to pray daily, remembering particularly the members of your class;
- to worship regularly with the gathered community as we celebrate our faith and encourage one another;
- to extend the love of God in the classroom;
- to live in ways that demonstrate God's love and mercy for all people and creation;
- to invite others to follow God's way in companionship with Jesus.

We promise as you begin this ministry
- to support you with our prayers, our money, and our actions;
- to provide teacher training;
- to supply curriculum material and resources for the classroom;
- to recognize that you are working on behalf of all the members of the congregation;
- to show our appreciation of your work.

On behalf of the Christian Education Committee _____, 19____

_____ Chairperson _____ Secretary

_____

I, _____ profess my belief in God our Creator, in Jesus Christ our Savior, and in the Holy Spirit our teacher and guide. I commit myself to share in the spiritual nurture of God's people and to develop my God-given gift of teaching. I hereby accept the call to teach _____ in the Sunday school of _____ Church, from _____ to _____

_____
Signature

_____ _____
Address   Phone

CHAPTER THREE
RECOGNITION, DEVELOPMENT, AND SUPPORT

- **Before Starting**
- **At the Beginning of the Work**
- **Throughout the Term**
- **At the End of the Term**
- **At the End of the Time of Service**
- **Can You Fire a Teacher?**

Then Jesus went around teaching from village to village. Calling the Twelve to him, he sent them out two by two and gave them authority over evil spirits. . . .
The apostles gathered around Jesus and reported to him all they had done and taught. Then, because so many people were coming and going that they did not even have a chance to eat, he said to them, "Come with me by yourselves to a quiet place and get some rest."
(Mark 6:6b-7, 30-31 NIV)

Think again of the football team mentioned at the beginning of the last chapter. As you know, it is important to recruit the best players possible for each position on a team. But just doing a good job of recruiting will not make a good team, let alone an effective one. Players have to work hard as individuals to be physically and mentally fit for the games, they have to practice together to refine their plays and develop strategies; they have to be well coached and supported as they play.

The same principles apply to Sunday school teachers. The purpose of education in your church will not be fulfilled if you don't provide teachers with recognition, support, and opportunities for development. Another of the top complaints of volunteers is the lack of recognition and support for their work. How would you like it if, once you were recruited as a teacher, you were handed the curriculum material, patted on the back, and told to "go to it" without any further contact from anyone in the Christian education network of the church? This happens all too often in congregations—once "gotten," forgotten. If you refer to the scripture passage at the beginning of this chapter, you will notice that Jesus did not just choose his disciples and then leave them to their own devices. He provided instructions; he acknowledged that they worked hard; and he listened to reports of what they had done. Congregations can do no less for their teachers today.

A group of several hundred people, recently asked to list the positive and negative aspects of working as a volunteer in the church (particularly as teachers), gave these responses:

Positive Aspects of Volunteering

- **had a clear job description**
- **knew what I had to do and that I was trusted and free to do it**
- **got feedback on what I did**
- **got support from other teachers and staff, a sense of being in it together**
- **had a sense of doing something worthwhile, feeling part of God's plan**
- **received recognition for my talents and a joyful opportunity to use them**
- **learned a lot and developed deeper understandings**
- **liked the people I worked with**
- **could help draw others out to examine their faith**

Negative Aspects of Volunteering

- **someone else made the decisions without consulting me**
- **was left completely on my own; a book was shoved in my hand**
- **didn't know how to do the job, and no one told me**
- **didn't know anything about the other teachers and what they were doing or about the people in the class**
- **no budget for supplies, books, pictures, and so on**
- **no one to turn to for help, ideas, answers, and resources**

The suggestions in this chapter are intended to help you create a working environment for volunteer teachers that will produce positive comments from teachers and students and faithful results for your educational ministry. Such an environment makes recruitment easier. People are more willing to volunteer when they know the working environment is stimulating and supportive.

Teachers need different kinds of training, recognition, and support at different times during their volunteer service, so let's look at this topic chronologically.

BEFORE STARTING

Refine the Job Description: Adjust to Special Needs and Gifts

It would be best for teachers to meet together as soon after they have all been recruited as possible and before the dedication service in late spring or early fall. They need this opportunity to review their job descriptions, to ask questions about it, and to make any appropriate adjustments. For example, someone may ask for funds to attend a workshop on music in the church rather than one on teaching in the church, feeling the program would benefit more from the music training he or she would receive.

Find out also if there are special needs among the teachers and make plans to respond to them. Some of the teachers may be single parents or have spouses on shift work and may need help with babysitting when attending teachers' meetings or workshops. Someone may need to be in a room without steps, without an echo, with a piano, near a washroom, and so on.

Observe the Class and Meet with the Retiring Teachers

It would be helpful if teachers could observe their future classes in action before this meeting and to talk with the present teachers after the class, perhaps over lunch provided by the Christian education committee.

The new teachers could share their reactions at the meeting and ask questions that arise from the experience. If they can't observe the classes before the meeting, try to make arrangements for them to do so at this time. This experience helps the new teachers know something about the teaching style the classes were used to before, the group feeling, and what the individual members are like. Having observed these, they can begin to think about the class and plan appropriately. Of course, the class probably won't be exactly the same when the new term begins. Some people drop out or shift to other classes, but the new teacher will still have had some exposure to the class.

Get to Know the Other Teachers

Make sure that there is time at this first meeting for teachers to get to know one another. Have a refreshment time, so that they can talk personally and informally, but also take time for teachers to share why they decided to teach, their hopes and fears as teachers, what they think they have to offer, and where they will need help. If you have team-teaching in your Sunday school, the teams may want to discuss how to deal with this information; for instance, if one teacher on the team is afraid to discipline "mouthy" children, how will the teammates help? If you don't have team-teaching, have a general discussion about the best way to work together, using everyone's gifts to help. For example, if one teacher offers a talent in drama, other teachers may ask him or her to help out in their classes once in a while.

Get Acquainted with the Facilities, Equipment, and Supplies

This meeting can be an opportunity for getting to know about things as well as people. If you have a complex Christian education facility, the new teachers may need to have a tour to know where everything is—kitchen, washrooms, audio-visual cupboard or room, supply depot, library, classrooms, assembly areas. If you have a small area for Christian education, you may only need to look through the supply cupboard. Teachers could then note what needs to be purchased to help them with their work or what they and others could collect—such as magazines, plastic containers, and egg cartons. Have a display of the most helpful resource books available for teachers—Bible dictionaries, craft books, and so on—and encourage people to borrow and use them.

If it seems appropriate at this meeting, have a hands-on time in which teachers get a chance to mix paints, use film projectors and computers, and experiment with other resources.

Prepare a Lesson

It may be best to work on lesson preparation just before the Sunday school term begins. Teachers may then be feeling the time pressure more and be ready to concentrate on preparation. So if you have your first teacher's meeting in the spring, you may want to wait until early fall to have the session on lesson preparation.

During the meeting, have the teachers group themselves according to departments, teams, age groupings, or whatever is suitable, to plan their first lesson. A leader experienced in lesson planning (an experienced teacher in the congregation or an outside resource person) should explain the process and then lead the teachers step-by-step through planning their first session—including background reading, preparation of materials, and room set-up. You can use this process whether teachers use printed curriculum or develop their own. The teachers could share their plans and give suggestions to one another. The superintendent or coordinators could respond to questions and concerns and make plans to provide further help to teachers who need it.

Meet with Parents and/or Class Participants

Have an informal teacher and student gathering in late spring or early fall. Parents, children, youth, adults, and their leaders could be invited for coffee and muffins before church or for lemonade and cookies afterward. People could gather into classes, introduce themselves, and get acquainted by talking about their favorite foods, television shows, Bible stories, and so on. The teacher could ask class participants what their hopes and fears are for the Sunday school class this year, and the teacher could share his or hers. They could all talk about how to prevent their fears and fulfill their hopes.

Teachers of young children might like to hear the views of parents at this meeting and make some commitment to continue communicating with them through letters, phone calls, visits, or meetings.

AT THE BEGINNING OF THE WORK

Provide Support

Most of us can probably think of situations in which we tried something new—riding a bicycle or learning to ride a different kind of bicycle, ten speed or two-seater—and remember our lack of confidence and our need for coaching in the mechanics and support and encouragement as we developed our skills. Teachers, starting out, often feel the same way whether they've taught before, but in a different setting with a different class, or whether they've never taught before. So it is important for the department coordinators, the Sunday school superintendent, a Christian education committee member, and the Christian education director to provide support at the beginning of the church year. They could do this by calling teachers a week before their first class to find out how their plans are coming and what resources, supplies, or equipment they may need or if they need help with setting up their rooms. These people's arrival at the church early on the first Sunday of classes lets the teachers know that help is at hand for finding supplies and equipment, answering questions, and giving support and reassurance. After class, speak to each teacher personally or by phone to see how the first session went and to find out what help is needed for the second.

Provide Coaching

It might also be helpful for a brand new teacher to have an experienced teacher observe and assist in the first few classes and then give supportive feedback and suggestions. A new teacher might need as much as three months of weekly coaching and follow up. More experienced teachers may need intensive support only for the first two or three weeks.

Teachers' Meeting

The first monthly teachers' meeting is a time when teachers share the highs and lows of teaching, sympathize and rejoice with one another, pass on helpful hints, and identify what they want to learn and do in future meetings.

THROUGHOUT THE TERM

Regular Feedback

Teachers may not need to have conversations in as much depth as they did at the beginning of the term, but they still need ongoing feedback about their work. A common complaint of volunteers is that they did not have a leader or supervisor or official person to be accountable to and to receive support from in an ongoing way.

The Sunday school superintendent or department coordinator (or whoever is appropriate) should try to speak briefly with every teacher each week to see how things are going. He or she might, at other times, drop into class for a while or even videotape it and talk about it with the teacher. This ongoing contact helps teachers feel appreciated for fulfilling an important job and enables coordinators to learn about problems quickly so that they may take the necessary steps to alleviate the situation early.

Help with Equipment and Supplies

It is a great support to teachers to have a person responsible for ordering supplies, maintaining the supply cupboard and equipment, keeping the library in order, setting up heavy tables and machinery, and so on. There may be one or two people in your congregation who would enjoy providing this kind of support for your education ministry.

Budget

Having a reasonable budget for books, equipment, supplies, decorating, workshops, and so on is good for teacher morale. One group of young teachers couldn't even get their church stewards to give them money for paint to spruce up the dingy furnace room where the Sunday school met. You can imagine the level of their spirits.

Back-up Volunteers

Teachers may want to go on special trips as part of their class studies. The recruiting committee can help find volunteers to prepare permission slips, to phone parents, and to arrange for volunteer drivers. Back-up support of this nature frees leaders to spend their time and energy on what they do best—teaching.

Regular Teachers' Meetings

It is best to have these meetings at the same time each month (or whatever frequency is appropriate) so that people can plan ahead. However, you may have to change around to meet everyone's needs. The time and place could be arranged to suit the life-style of the leaders—breakfast before church, lunch after church, an evening through the week—at the church, in homes, or in retreat centers. It is important to meet even if there are only two or three teachers in your congregation.

All meetings should provide time for leaders to share their joys and sorrows in their personal and teaching lives. They need to hear what is working well in other teachers' classes and to help one another solve problems. They need to study scripture and pray together.

Most meetings should have an information sharing or training component. Teachers can pass on articles, books, and audiovisual resources they have found helpful. They can teach one another. Someone with gifts in instrumental music can lead a workshop on how to apply it to Sunday school. Or a teacher who has done a lot of work on a particular Bible passage related to the curriculum can lead a session about it. Outside resource people could also come and give leadership on topics of interest. The topics should be decided by the teachers and may cover any number of subject areas—spiritual life, pastoral care in the class, biblical studies, working with particular age groups, creative expression, group dynamics, social justice issues, teaching methods. Teachers also need support from the superintendent or coordinator to plan how they will apply their new learnings to their teaching. They may also want or be asked to attend an annual retreat and/or an annual trip to a lay training center for workshops.

Report to the Congregation

Members of the congregation cannot recognize the work of volunteer teachers unless they are informed. Here are some ways to do this:

- **Have classes take part in the worship service—leading in a prayer they wrote, teaching a song or hymn, offering their outreach project, and so on;**
- **Have displays of class projects in the church or the narthex;**
- **Have teachers report the highlights of their monthly meetings, retreats, or workshops during announcement time in worship, in the worship bulletin, and the church newsletter;**

- **Have students write stories of what's happening in their classes for the bulletin and newsletter;**
- **Make regular reports to the Christian education committee and the church board on the work of the teachers in the education program.**

These reports might also help in future recruiting. Some church members may have been so intrigued by such presentations that they may decide to teach.

AT THE END OF THE TERM
Evaluation

At the end of every term of service, or even more frequently, teachers should have their work evaluated and, in turn, evaluate the Sunday school system, no matter how small. A good teacher will want to know what his or her strengths are and where she or he needs to learn more. A good superintendent or coordinator will want to know if the teacher achieved his or her personal goals; whether the goals for education in the church were met; how teacher recruitment, training, and support could be improved; and where the educational program could be beneficially changed. The form on page 37 can help with this process.

Sometimes people balk at the idea of evaluating volunteers, but the process of evaluating conveys to the volunteer and to the congregation that teaching in the church is important work that must be done faithfully and well. People worry about giving feedback about performance. We have a problem if we in the church (who are supposed to know that we are accepted for who we are, despite our shortcomings) can't be told that we need to develop our God-given gifts more or if we can't celebrate the great things we're doing with God's help. Of course, we need not only to hear evaluations, but also to act on them. If teachers see their suggestions acted upon, they feel that their opinions count.

Thank You Notes and Gifts

Teachers will feel recognized and appreciated if they receive thank you notes from the Sunday school superintendent, the Christian education committee, or the church board. Some churches also write to the families of teachers to let them know how much their family member's gifts were valued. A small gift, possibly a book related to faith and/or to teaching in the church, might also be appropriate.

A Service of Recognition or Thanksgiving

Recognize the work of volunteer teachers in a worship service at the end of the Sunday school year. The whole congregation is involved in lifting up and celebrating before God the valuable ministry of these people.

A Thank You Reception or Banquet

Some congregations have an annual evening banquet for all the education leaders in the church. Something simpler, such as a reception with refreshments after the service of recognition or thanksgiving, serves the same purpose.

AT THE END OF THE TIME OF SERVICE
Exit Interview

At the end of their time of service, volunteer teachers deserve an exit interview with the superintendent or coordinator and a member of the Christian education committee. This would be a time for the teachers to express their regrets and appreciations and their joys and sorrows in educational ministry in your congregation. This is a time when they could make comments and suggestions about the system that they might not put forward if they were staying on. See the form on page 39. The interviewers would express thanks to the teacher(s) and discuss where they might want to serve now in the congregation (if appropriate). This information would be passed on to suitable committees.

Letter of Reference

Volunteer work is often seriously considered when people are applying for paid employment. Offering a letter of reference to retiring teachers indicates that their work was important and valued.

Special Recognition

The contributions of retiring teachers should be noted in a worship service, banquet, reception, bulletin, or newsletter.

CAN YOU FIRE A TEACHER?

Yes and no. The word *fire* expresses the action too pejoratively. And so to *firing* the answer is no. To finding a job that better suits a person's talents, the answer is yes. All people have gifts, but sometimes they undertake jobs that don't use them and don't serve God and others. Therefore, it's necessary to find a better match. Thinking about an unsuitable teacher in this way is less rejecting.

When it is clear that someone is not able to teach, the one who needs to take action will have the "support" of a job description, a term of service, and a regular evaluation process. The superintendent, or an appropriate person, would need to meet with this teacher as soon as the problem appears. The teacher should be asked how he or she thinks the teaching is going. Often the teacher may express dissatisfaction. This would give you the opportunity to point out what talents this person has shown and to offer her or him a job that better suits his or her talents.

If the teacher is not aware that his or her behavior is not appropriate, you may have to refer to the job description, noting for example that instead of relating well with the class, this teacher yells at the children 60 percent of the time or that a teacher, instead of preparing lessons that include creative activities, only talks to the children and expects them to sit still. You may need to give the teacher an opportunity to change his or her behavior. But if there is no change, note at the end of the term that the time of service is over and that there is a job in another part of the church's work that needs that person's gifts.

This can be a painful process, but it is even more dehumanizing and demoralizing to leave someone in a job he or she is not suited for. It may be hard for the person to admit that teaching isn't his or her thing, but by acknowledging this, the person gains an opportunity to find out what his or her real gifts are. Having an unsuitable teacher in a class can turn the members off Christian education. That's like putting millstones around their necks, and we want to do all we can to prevent that—even to the point of redirecting people away from teaching.

This may seem like a negative note on which to draw to a close, but it is really positive. Matching gifts and talents is important work—so important that when we make mistakes we must correct them for the sake of the person and of the work. We can't just let things stay as they are as if it didn't matter. It does matter.

You *can* find teachers—that's what this book promised, and it's true. Recruiting, training, and supporting the best possible teachers for your educational ministry are arts and ministries in themselves—and call for work. Make the work pay off by approaching it the right way. The process and ideas presented here are intended to give you a way to build a meaningful program of Christian education in your congregation. Start now talking with others about the dreams for your educational ministry and the gifted people right in your congregation who can make them happen. Believe it: You *can* find teachers.

FURTHER READING

Adolph, Val. *Volunteers and the Church: From Potential to Action* (Delta, British Columbia: William A. Fletcher Publishing, 1985).

Foster, Charles R. *The Ministry of the Volunteer Teachers* (Nashville: Abingdon Press, 1986).

Wilson, Marlene. *How to Mobilize Church Volunteers* (Minneapolis: Augsburg Publishing House, 1983).

ONGOING EVALUATION

Keep in mind your relationship with students, your grasp and interpretation of lesson material, and your own and the students' spiritual growth as you reflect on these questions.

Personal

1. I am satisfied with my work in this teaching ministry position in the following ways:

2. I am not satisfied with my work in the following ways:

3. I would like to build on my positive experiences by:

4. I would like to resolve my dissatisfaction by:

Students

1. I think the students appreciate my teaching ministry in the following areas:

2. I think the students do not appreciate my ministry in the following areas:

3. I plan to build on the positive by:

4. I plan to change the following:

Sunday School System

1. I feel recognized, supported, and helped by the Sunday school system, teammates, the superintendent, the Christian education committee, and so on in the following ways:

2. I do not feel recognized, supported, and helped by the Sunday school system, teammates, the superintendent, the Christian education committee, and so on in the following ways:

3. I would like to see the following changes:

REPORT AND EVALUATION OF A VOLUNTEER TEACHING MINISTRY
(Exit Interview)

Name _____ Telephone # _____

Title of Ministry Position _____

Term of the Position: From _____ to _____

1. This educational ministry position has been satisfying for me because:

2. The major frustrations in this educational position have been:

3. I used the following skills in this ministry position:

4. The training I received for this teaching position included:

5. I felt supported in this position in the following ways:

6. I received the following resources, which assisted me in this position :

7. I would have been able to do this teaching ministry better if:

8. The highlights of this ministry for me have been:

9. The major achievements of this ministry include:

10. A person following me in this teaching ministry position needs to know:

Please rate each of the following as they enabled you to do this ministry effectively and faithfully by placing and "X" in the appropriate column.

	Outstanding	Average	Inadequate
11. The way in which the position was interpreted and explained to me before I began	☐	☐	☐
12. The training I received for doing the ministry	☐	☐	☐
13. The support I received from the church	☐	☐	☐
14. The challenge and responsibility I felt in doing this ministry	☐	☐	☐
15. The sense of importance the church places on this ministry	☐	☐	☐

The following are about your future volunteer ministries. Please indicate your interest by placing an "X" in the appropriate column.

	Very Interested	Somewhat Interested	Would Like to Know More	No Interest
16. A new volunteer ministry position:				
a) in my church	☐	☐	☐	☐
b) in my community	☐	☐	☐	☐
c) in my denomination	☐	☐	☐	☐
d) in an ecumenical setting	☐	☐	☐	☐

17. Specific volunteer ministry opportunities I would like to explore:

18. Factors in my situation that would influence my next volunteer ministry position:

   Schedule:

   Transportation:

   Other:

19. Additional comments:

Take Your Light out from Under a Bushel

Come and Build the Body of Christ

Tomorrow Depends on You Today!

Come and Build the Body of Christ

You Could Be the Spark

Tomorrow Depends on You Today!

TEACH: PREPARE TODAY'S DISCIPLES!

Take Your Light out from Under a Bushel

You Can Make a Difference!

YOUR GIFT CAN GO A LONG WAY

You Can Make a Difference!

You Could Be the Spark

Take Your Light out from Under a Bushel

TEACH: PREPARE TODAY'S DISCIPLES!

Take Your Light out from Under a Bushel

You Can Make a Difference!

You Could Be the Spark *You Could Be the Spark*

YOUR GIFT CAN GO A LONG WAY

Tomorrow Depends on You Today!

Tomorrow Depends on You Today!

Come and Build the Body of Christ

TEACH: PREPARE TODAY'S DISCIPLES!

YOUR GIFT CAN GO A LONG WAY

YOUR GIFT CAN GO A LONG WAY

YOUR GIFT CAN GO A LONG WAY

YOUR GIFT CAN GO A LONG WAY